CENGAGE Learning

Drama for Students, Volume 34

Project Editor: Kristin B. Mallegg Rights Acquisition and Management: Ashley Maynard Composition: Evi Abou-El-Seoud

Manufacturing: Rita Wimberley

Imaging: John Watkins

Digital Content Production: Edna Shy © 2017 Gale, Cengage Learning

For product information and technology assistance, contact us at **Gale Customer Support, 1-800-877-4253**.

For permission to use material from this text or product, submit all requests online at **www.cengage.com/permissions**.

Further permissions questions can be emailed to **permissionrequest@cengage.com**
While every effort has been made to ensure the reliability of the information presented in this publication, Gale, a part of Cengage Learning, does not guarantee the accuracy of the data contained herein. Gale accepts no payment for listing; and inclusion in the publication of any organization, agency, institution, publication, service, or individual does not imply endorsement of the editors or publisher. Errors brought to the attention of the publisher and verified to the satisfaction of the publisher will be corrected in future editions.

Gale
27500 Drake Rd.
Farmington Hills, MI, 48331-3535

ISBN-13: 978-1-4103-2832-8
ISSN 1094-9232

This title is also available as an e-book.
ISBN-13: 978-1-4103-9271-8
ISBN-10: 1-4103-9271-8
Contact your Gale, a part of Cengage Learning sales

representative for ordering information.

Printed in Mexico
1 2 3 4 5 6 7 21 20 19 18 17

The God of Carnage

Yasmina Reza 2006

Introduction

In Yasmina Reza's *The God of Carnage*, first produced in 2006, two couples meet to make peace after a playground fight between their sons leaves one boy with two broken teeth. Though the afternoon begins with espresso, small talk, and a spirit of compromise, the Reilles and the Vallons are soon consumed by the same animal rage that set their sons against each other. Within an hour, there are tears, vomit, tantrums, name calling, and violence, as the conventions of polite society break down to reveal the brutality beneath the polished middleclass exteriors of Alain, Annette, Véronique, and Michel. Winner of the Molière Award, the Laurence Olivier Award, and three Tony Awards, including Best Play, Best Director, and Best Leading Actress, *The God of Carnage* takes delight in the collapse of civilization.

Author Biography

Reza Was Born May 1, 1959, In Paris, France. She Attended The University Of Paris X In Nanterre, Where She Studied Sociology And Theater. After Enrolling In The Jacques Lecocq International Drama School In Paris, She Began A Short-Lived Acting Career. Struggling To Find Work As An Actress, She Began To Write Plays Instead.

In 1987 her first play, *Conversations after a Burial* (*Conversations après un enterrement*) was produced and won the coveted Molière Award. Her second play, *The Winter Crossing* (*La traversée de l'hiver*), was produced in 1989, for which Reza won a second Molière Award. International success and recognition came with the production of her third play, '*Art*,' which debuted in Paris in 1994 before opening in London's West End in 1996 and on Broadway in New York City in 1998. '*Art*' won the Molière Award in 1994, the Tony Award for Best Play in 1998, and the Laurence Olivier Award for Best Comedy that same year. She followed this success with *The Unexpected Man* (*L'homme du hasard*) in 1995, *Life x 3* (*Trois versions de la vie*) in 2000, and *A Spanish Play* (*Une pièce espagnole*) in 2004 and embarked upon a career as a novelist. She spent a year with French president Nicolas Sarkozy following his 2007 election campaign. Her book on the experience, *Dawn, Dusk, or Night* (*L'aube, le soir ou le nuit*), published in 2007, was wildly popular in France.

The God of Carnage (*Le dieu du carnage*) premiered in Zurich, Switzerland, in 2006. It then showed in Paris in 2007, London in 2008, and New York City in 2009. Reza became the first female playwright to win two Laurence Olivier Awards when *The God of Carnage* won for Best Comedy in 2009. That same year she became the first female playwright to win two Tony Awards for Best Play. In addition, Marcia Gay Harden won the Tony Award for Best Leading Actress in a Play for her portrayal of Vèronique (changed to Veronica in the American production), and Matthew Warchus won the Tony Award for Best Director of a Play.

Reza is reticent toward the media, and little is known of her life outside her writing career. In *The Plays of Yasmina Reza on the English and American Stage*, Amanda Giguere writes of the mystery surrounding Reza's personal life: "Although Reza does occasionally give interviews, she has been known to avoid the press, and has even admitted to warping the truth when speaking to reporters."

The God Of Carnage begins as two couples in their forties—the Vallons and the Reilles—meet for the first time to discuss a violent incident between their sons. They sit facing each other in the Vallons's living room, which features a coffee table stacked with art books and a vase of tulips. Vèronique Vallon reads a statement about the incident aloud for the group: following an argument at the Aspirant Dunant Gardens, eleven-year-old Ferdinand Reille, armed with a stick, struck Bruno Vallon in the face. The blow caused Bruno to lose two teeth and sustain nerve damage in his gums.

Alain Reille objects to the phrase "armed." Vèronique suggests, "furnished" instead. They agree on this terminology, and Vèronique corrects the statement. The couples thank each other for their willingness to settle the matter among themselves like adults. As Vèronique says: "Fortunately, there is still such a thing as the art of co-existence, is there not?"

Annette Reille asks after Bruno's affected nerve, and the Vallons explain that the recovery will be complicated as his teeth are still growing, making permanent implants impossible until he is at least eighteen years old. After Annette compliments the tulips, Vèronique tells her that Bruno refused to identify Ferdinand as his attacker at first. Michel Vallon, her husband, corrects her assessment that this is not necessarily admirable, as he did not want to be known as a snitch to his friends. Annette asks how they found out Ferdinand's name. The couple explains that they told Bruno that Ferdinand must be held accountable or else he might strike again and that surely his parents would want to know.

Media Adaptations

- The God of Carnage, adapted in a film titled Carnage by Roman Polanski and starring Jodie Foster, Kate Winslet, Christoph Waltz, and John C. Reilly, was produced by SBS Productions and distributed by Sony Picture Classics in 2011.

Alain's phone vibrates. He takes the call. He tells the man on the line, Maurice, that a report was published in *Le Monde* claiming that a pharmaceutical drug, Antril, has been discovered to cause a range of serious side effects. Alain tells Maurice in sharp tones that this discovery is extremely inconvenient to them and to find out where else this report has been published. He hangs up, apologizing to the room. He tells the Vallons that he is a lawyer. Michel is a wholesaler of household goods. Véronique is a writer who works part-time at a bookshop. A specialist in African studies, her book on the tragedy in Darfur will soon be published.

Annette asks if Bruno is their only child. Véronique tells her that Bruno has a nine-year-old sister, Camille, who is angry with her father for letting her hamster out. Michel explains that he hated the hamster, which made incessant noise throughout the night in its cage. Bruno could not get his needed rest and recovery with the hamster carrying on, and since Michel had always despised it, he decided finally to act. He left it outside in the gutter, thinking it would run free. Instead it sat paralyzed. In the morning it had vanished.

Véronique asks what Annette does for a living. Annette is in wealth management. Véronique suggests that Ferdinand apologize to Bruno. Annette agrees, but Alain claims that Ferdinand does not understand the gravity of the situation: he is still a child. Véronique says he is not a baby, but Michel counters that he is not an adult either.

Michel offers the couple something to drink and insists the Reilles try the *clafoutis* his wife made. Alain asks Michel about his job selling household hardware, and Michel admits there is not much money in the business but it offers some stability. Annette cuts in suddenly to ask why Michel left the hamster in the gutter once he realized it was frozen with fear. Michel explains that he absolutely will not touch rodents. He had tipped it out of its cage onto the street and could not bring himself to pick it up with his bare hands. Véronique returns from the kitchen with the *clafoutis*, espresso, and water. When Annette asks what is in the *clafoutis*, she is taken aback when Véronique answers that there are apples and pears. The dessert is traditionally made with cherries, but this variation is Michel's mother's recipe. They try it and express delight at the taste. The secret ingredient is gingerbread crumbs.

Alain says that at least something good has come of the incident: a new recipe for *clafoutis*. Véronique takes offense, saying: "I'd have preferred it if it hadn't cost my son two teeth." Alain's phone rings, saving him from the awkward moment. Speaking to Maurice once more, he asks how long the company knew about the side effects and why they did not recall the product. He hangs up, dialing another number. As he speaks, he wolfs down *clafoutis*. He explains to a man named Serge that Maurice and the company have known about the dangerous side effects for two years. He says rather than reply immediately, they will acknowledge the report only if the story spreads. He hangs up, rejoining the conversation.

Speaking of the *clafoutis* recipe, Véronique

mentions that Michel's mother must have an operation on her knee. The Reilles compliment the Vallons on their openness toward reconciliation. Annette brushes this aside: "Not at all. How many parents standing up for their children become infantile themselves?" Then, they immediately begin to argue over whether Ferdinand has disfigured Bruno. Véronique says yes. Annette says no. Michel says he has been disfigured temporarily. He wants to arrange a meeting for the boys, where Ferdinand can apologize. The couples wonder if they should be present or not.

When the Vallons ask if Ferdinand feels like apologizing, the Reilles are firm that his emotions toward the situation do not matter. Alain says: "Madame, our son is a savage. To hope for any kind of spontaneous repentance would be fanciful." The Reilles prepare to leave. They ask the Vallons to bring Bruno to their home around seven-thirty. Michel objects. He thinks Ferdinand should come to them, as Bruno is the victim. Véronique insists both parents be present. In that case, Alain says as his phone vibrates again, the reconciliation cannot take place tonight. He answers, telling the person on the other end that there is no evidence of wrongdoing, then hangs up. When Véronique expresses doubt that the apology will be effective, since the Reilles seem convinced of their son's savagery, Alain tells the Vallons that obviously they are better parents than he and his wife but that they cannot expect them to rise to their level immediately. Michel tries to urge everyone to calm down. Annette agrees, and the couple accepts Michel's offer to stay for another coffee while they try to work things out.

While they wait on coffee, Annette peruses the art books on the table. When Michel returns with the coffee, they try to understand the nature of the boys' argument. Bruno would not let Ferdinand join his gang. Michel did not know that Bruno had a gang. He thinks this is great news. He had a gang when he was young. Alain says he had a gang of his own as well. Michel is overcome with a memory of fighting and beating another boy who was bigger than he. When he describes the altercation, Véronique scolds him. She wants to personally speak to Ferdinand. Alain says she can if she wants, but he doubts it will have any effect. They get into a spat over each other's phrasing, which Annette tries to break up by agreeing to bring Ferdinand over that night. Alain's phone rings.

He tells the person on the other end not to take the drug off the market, or else the company will be admitting liability for the side effects. He says they will think of the victims later. He urges them not to make any statements and then phones a colleague. He tells him to write a press release denying all accusations. When he gets off the phone, Michel tells him pharmaceutical companies have no morals, only an eye for profit. The men argue, with Alain belittling Michel's career selling doorknobs and toilet fittings.

Véronique cuts in to their sarcastic exchange to ask if the Reilles plan on punishing Ferdinand. Annette complains that she feels sick. As the Vallons try to help Annette, Alain calls his office but cannot find Serge. Annette says they will punish their son in a way they see fit. Michel agrees. Véronique disagrees—she thinks it is their business as well. Alain answers a call. Annette shouts at him to hang up the phone and join the conversation.

Alain says how dare she shout; Serge heard everything she said, and he is only here as a favor to her. Annette says she is about to vomit and begins to panic. Alain tries to talk her down, calling her Woof-woof, his pet name for her. She tells him to get away from her, sick of his disinterest in their domestic life. She vomits everywhere: on Alain, on the art books, all over the table. Chaos ensues. Alain shouts at her for not going to the bathroom to vomit. Véronique grabs a bowl for her in case it happens again. Michel swears it cannot be the *clafoutis*; it is nerves—a panic attack over her responsibilities as a mother. Annette half-listens to him, vomiting weakly into the bowl.

One of the art books ruined is out of print, and Michel works to salvage what he can of his wife's precious possession. Annette and Alain go to the bathroom to clean themselves up while Michel and Véronique clean the living room, spraying perfume and attempting to clean the table. They agree that the Reilles are awful, but Véronique scolds Michel for continually siding with them. They make fun of Annette's pet name, Woof-woof, until Alain interrupts them—having entered the room unseen—to defend the pet name. He hands them the hair dryer to help save the art books. They reconcile, the Vallons explaining that they call each other "darjeeling," which is just as silly. When Annette returns to the living room, Véronique apologizes for caring more about her book than about Annette's health.

The couples return to discussing their sons. Annette suggests that name calling, which Bruno engaged in before the attack, is another form of violence. If attacked, people naturally defend themselves. Michel tells her that she seems to have more energy now that she has vomited. He is admonished for being crude, but he argues that he will not allow the children to pull him down to their level. Alain and Annette say they must leave, and Véronique tells them to go, because she gives up.

Michel's mother calls. The doctors have given her Antril—the same medication Alain has been discussing—for her blood pressure. He tells her to stop taking it immediately. Michel stops the couple on the way out to tell them that it is clear from their behavior where Ferdinand gets his attitude. Annette fires back that at least they did not murder an innocent hamster, leaving it shivering with fear in the gutter.

Véronique agrees wholeheartedly, to Michel's shock. She thinks the hamster must have met a terrible fate. Michel defends himself. He thought the hamster would be happy to be free. Besides, he is terrified of rodents, snakes, and anything close to the ground. Alain asks why Véronique did not go looking for the hamster. She says Michel kept what he had done a secret. It had disappeared by the time she went searching. Annette asks if he feels guilty.

Michel says no, that he is thrilled that it is gone. Annette counters that if Michel feels no guilt for murdering a hamster, why do the Vallons expect Ferdinand to feel guilt over beating Bruno?

Michel says he has had enough of these inane philosophical discussions. The truth is that he does not care: he is as uninterested as Alain. The meeting was Véronique's idea. Véronique says she is standing up for civilization. She begins to cry. Michel tries to comfort her unsuccessfully, before suggesting everyone take a drink of rum. Alain accepts the offer, forgetting his haste to leave. The Reilles take over comforting Véronique, and Alain admits that—like Michel—he had to be dragged to this meeting by his wife. Annette accepts a glass of rum, too. Véronique demands a drink, but Michel says no. They fight over the bottle until Michel relents. Michel tells them all that marriage and children ruin lives. Annette does not believe he means it, but Véronique assures her that he does. Alain pours himself another glass and takes a call. Annette complains loudly to the Vallons about Alain's excessive cell phone use. She says she will be sick again. Véronique hands her the basin in case she needs it. When he hangs up and sees Annette with the basin, he tells her that just because the Vallons have a miserable marriage does not mean they need to compete. Véronique starts to argue, but Alain's phone rings again. When he gets off the phone, he explains his philosophy toward the attack:

> They're young, they're kids, kids
> have always given each other a good

drubbing during break. It's a law of
life.... I believe in the god of
carnage. He has ruled,
uninterruptedly, since the dawn of
time.

Annette dryheaves but says that she is fine.
Alain lectures Véronique on the state of affairs in
the Congo, which he recently visited. When he
brings up Darfur, Michel tells Alain not to get her
started. Véronique throws herself, kicking and
punching, at her husband, until Alain pulls her off.
He says he is starting to like Véronique. Véronique
tells him she does not like him. After dryheaving
again, Annette continues to drink rum. Véronique
joins her and declares: "We're living in France
according to the principles of Western society.
What goes on in Aspirant Dunant Gardens reflects
the values of Western society!"

Michel asks if spousal abuse is one of those
principles. Alain says Michel should be flattered by
her attention. Annette and Véronique mock their
husbands for their boyhood gangs and the warrior
urges that keep them from being any practical help
at all around the house or with the children. Alain's
phone rings again. Annette grabs the phone from
him and drops it into the vase of tulips.

Annette and Véronique celebrate while Michel
and Alain panic. Michel grabs the phone and uses
the hair dryer to attempt to dry it. Alain tells
Annette she should be locked away: his whole life
was on that phone. Annette repeats this phrase,
mocking him. The men scramble to save the phone

while the women laugh cruelly and drink more rum. After a long minute of Michel's careful blow-drying, Alain tells him it is ruined. After a silence, Annette declares that she feels great. She believes a man who relies so heavily on an accessory appears weak. A man should wear his solitude proudly. Véronique says she has never been unhappier than she is at this moment. Alain slumps on the couch, defeated. The house phone rings.

Michel's mother has called back, asking about the medication. Michel hands the phone to Alain, demanding that he tell his mother everything. They talk, with Michel's mother mistakenly believing he is a doctor and Alain recommending she stop taking the medication at once. Michel takes the phone back and says good-bye. Annette asks if she should bring Ferdinand over tonight or not, though she personally believes there are wrongs on both sides. Véronique says she has had enough of Annette. She grabs Annette's handbag and throws it at the door. Annette cries for Alain to do something in a high-pitched voice, as if she were a little girl. Véronique mocks her. Alain gathers the pieces of his cell phone while Michel scolds Véronique for acting as if she has the high moral ground above them all. Annette tries to keep drinking, but Alain stops her. Véronique calls her a phony. Alain agrees, saying that Véronique is the only person involved who actually cares about the issue at hand and that her desire to make the world a fair, balanced place makes her less attractive to men and makes Michel depressed.

Véronique asks who cares what Alain likes in a woman, especially considering the way he conducts himself. Alain observes in the same tone that now she is yelling. Véronique asks if Annette yelled when she found out her son is a violent brute. The women start to taunt each other—calling their sons the same names their sons called each other before the fight. Annette pulls out the tulips from the vase and shreds them, making a great mess. She calls the flowers pathetic and declares this the worst day of her life as well.

After a stunned pause, Michel picks up Annette's glasses case from the floor and hands it to her. Alain starts to pick up flowers, but Michel tells him to stop. The phone rings. Véronique answers. Their daughter is on the phone asking about the hamster. Véronique assures her that they searched everywhere but that the hamster will survive on any number of things: leaves, acorns, worms, snails, even food from the trash. When she hangs up, Michel says that the hamster must be having a feast. Véronique says, flatly, no. After a silence, Michel asks, "What do we know?"

Didier Leglu

Didier was a boy whom Michel fought in single combat when he was the leader of his childhood gang. Michel remembers beating Didier with pride, as Didier was bigger than Michel.

Maurice

Maurice is Alain's client, who is panicking in light of a recent report that Antril, a drug that his company sells, causes ataxia and death. Alain has a very low opinion of Maurice.

Alain Reille

Alain is Ferdinand's father, Annette's husband, and a lawyer. While the couples talk, he takes calls from his client and colleagues over a recently published report that the client's pharmaceutical company produces a pill, Antril, which causes physically debilitating side effects. From the start, Alain urges his client not to admit any knowledge of the side effects, though the company has known of them for over two years. Alain tries to leave the Vallons's home several times, telling them that Annette can handle this problem as he is utterly incapable of helping in these domestic affairs. Alain admits that he believes in the god of carnage, and his attitude toward his son's attack on Bruno reflects this belief. While he and Michel see eye to eye about matters of boyhood aggression and adult masculinity, Alain and Véronique do not mix well. He calls her insistence on pursuing what is morally right and fair to be an inherently unattractive trait in a woman. He attempts to explain the Darfur situation to her—though she is an expert in the situation, with a book coming out on the subject. He approves of her only when she physically assaults her husband. Alain is an insensitive but authoritative presence in the argument, arguing in favor of the brutal nature of existence. He admits that he has no real interest in the outcome of the discussion, as he considers his son a savage incapable of understanding the consequences of his actions.

Annette Reille

Annette is Ferdinand's mother, Alain's second wife, and works in wealth management. She finds aspects of her husband's behavior, especially his views on domestic roles and his phone use, literally sickening: she vomits after arguing with him over their roles in the home as well as the calls he insists on taking throughout their conversation with the Vallons. After vomiting, she goes on the offensive —accusing Bruno of provoking Ferdinand into his violent outburst. At different times throughout the protracted argument, Annette is aligned with Alain, Michel, and Véronique against the others.

Ultimately, the room turns on her, with all three parents agreeing that she is a phony who does not actually care about the situation. She gets very drunk on rum with Véronique, though she retches several times into the bowl the Vallons have provided her each time her husband rants about gender roles or takes a phone call. She and Véronique mock their husbands for their delusions of masculinity until Véronique throws Annette's purse at the door and teases her cruelly for crying for Alain to help. Though Annette offers several times to bring her son over to apologize, this never provides an end to the debate.

Ferdinand Reille

Ferdinand is Alain and Annette's eleven-year-old son. After Bruno Vallon tells him he cannot be a member of Bruno's gang, Ferdinand strikes Bruno with a stick, knocking out two of his teeth. Though Annette is willing to bring Ferdinand to the Vallons's home so that he may apologize to Bruno, Alain maintains that Ferdinand is a savage who has no remorse for or understanding of his violent actions.

Serge

Serge is Alain's colleague, for whom he has a great deal of respect. Alain passes on the information Maurice provides him about the medication Antril to Serge throughout the play. He scolds his wife for shouting about Alain's incessant cell phone use when Serge can hear her.

Bruno Vallon

Bruno is the son of Michel and Véronique. The leader of a gang of boys, he insulted Ferdinand while the boys were playing at Aspirant Dunant Gardens. He called Ferdinand names and told him he could not join Bruno's gang. Ferdinand struck Bruno with a stick, causing significant facial swelling and breaking two of his teeth, one of which suffers nerve damage. Bruno will not give up the name of his attacker at first, unwilling to be seen as a snitch by his peers. It is only after Michel and Véronique convince him that it is the right thing to do that he admits that Ferdinand is the culprit.

Camille Vallon

Camille is the nine-year-old daughter of Véronique and Michel. After Michel leaves her hamster in the street, he attempts to convince Camille that it ran away. Camille does not believe her father, and during the play's events she is so angry with him that she will not speak to him. At the end of the play she calls her mother from her friend's house, asking if they have found her hamster. Véronique assures her that the hamster is happy to live in the wild and more than capable of taking care of itself.

Michel Vallon

Michel is Véronique's husband and Bruno's father. He is a wholesaler of home fixtures. Though he seems at first to be mild and companionable, he is, in fact, as disinterested in the proceedings of the meeting as Alain. He has a phobia of rodents that led him to release his daughter's hamster in the street, an unforgivable act of cruelty in the eyes of the gathered group as well as his daughter, who is not speaking to him. Like his son, he was the leader of a gang when he was a boy, and he recognizes Bruno's reluctance to identify Ferdinand as his attacker as concern over being considered a snitch, not because of any righteous sense of honor, as Véronique believes. Michel switches sides constantly throughout the conversation. His wife scolds him over his flip-flopping when they get a moment alone. When Annette dunks her husband's phone in the vase, he works desperately to save it—using the hair dryer on the individual pieces long after Alain has given up hope for its survival. Michel puts on a liberal act to match his wife's, which soon crumbles to reveal his true self. He finds Véronique's concern for doing what is right exhausting and believes that schoolyard fights are a fact of life. The wives tease him for speaking as if he is a warrior when he is really so scared of the hamster that he cannot pick it up from the street once it is obvious the animal is paralyzed with fear.

Michel Vallon's Mother

Michel's mother is preparing for an operation on her knee. Véronique serves her recipe for *clafoutis* with apples and pears to the group. When Michel discovers that her doctors have given her Antril to lower her blood pressure prior to the surgery, he tells her to stop taking it immediately, fearing the side effects. When she calls again, Michel puts Alain on the phone to tell her to stop taking her medication. She mistakes him for a doctor.

Véronique Vallon

Véronique is Michel's wife and Bruno's mother. She is a writer with a book on the Darfur tragedy coming out in January. She is a moral crusader, whose insistence that the apology between the boys be meaningful stalls the proceedings between the two couples and leads directly to their chaotic fight. Véronique is acknowledged by the end of the play as the only decent parent in the room, but no one especially likes her for her zealousness. Even Michel is desperate to avoid talk of Darfur—the area of her expertise—so that he will not have to hear her go on about the injustices there. This leads to Véronique's physically attacking her husband, revealing her to be the most violent of the group. Véronique believes in civility and Western society, though she is more concerned about her rare art books than she is over Annette's health after Annette is suddenly sick. It is important to her that Ferdinand apologize sincerely, and she cannot accept Alain's belief that his son is a savage who is sorry for nothing. She forms a brief bond with Annette over their husbands' ridiculous pretensions at masculinity, which is shattered after she throws Annette's handbag at the door and mocks her crying to her husband for help. When Alain condescends to Véronique about the political landscape of Darfur as well as how an attractive woman should behave, she tells him she could not care less what he thinks, as he is addicted to his phone and a terrible father. At the end of the play, Véronique reassures her daughter so effectively that even Michel believes her lie that the hamster will thrive in the wild.

Themes

Childhood

A main concern of *The God of Carnage* is the question of childhood. At eleven years old, can Ferdinand be held responsible for his actions, be expected to apologize sincerely, or even comprehend what he has done? Is Ferdinand's attack symptomatic of a maladjusted personality? Or is this violence, like Bruno's gang, a part of childhood? While the parents attempt to answer these questions, they reveal themselves to be as violent, unapologetic, and capable of spontaneous brutality as their sons. They argue, mutter sarcastic slights against one another, interrupt, shout, and cry. They show no self-discipline, gulping down cake, rum, and cigars—indulging in vices like kids in a candy store. They tease, betray, and show no pity for their partners while treating the other couple with contempt and condescension. Their capacity for cruelty seems endless, and when they finally do collapse, it seems more from physical exhaustion than the exhaustion of their ability to find fault with one another. Annette vomits and cries out for protection in a little girl's voice. Véronique bullies those weaker than she is with physical violence, beating her husband and throwing Annette's purse. After Annette breaks Alain's favorite toy (his phone), he pouts, refusing to interact with the others anymore, while Michel tries to placate everyone at once, as if she were an anxious child of combative parents. Yet Michel, too, has shown a child's heartlessness in his selfish disposal of the hamster. The adults are too immature themselves to solve the issue of their sons' immaturity, but their childishness raises more troubling questions. At forty, are these adults responsible for their own behavior? Can they say sorry and mean it? Do they understand what they have done?

Topics for Further Study

- Read Nancy Werlin's young-adult novel *The Rules of Survival* (2006). How does Alain's theory of the god of carnage apply to Werlin's novel? How do Matt's rules of survival differ from Alain's? What similarities and differences can you find between Matt, Ferdinand, and Bruno? Organize your answers into an essay.

- In small groups, act out an excerpt from the play. One member of your group should act as the director, giving the actor's notes on their performances and filming the scene for presentation to the class. Free video editing software is available at EDpuzzle.com.

- Choose one of the four main characters to examine more closely. Create a blog dedicated to this character in which you make a minimum of five posts exploring their beliefs, behavior, career, patterns of speech, and relationship to the other characters. Include photos of actors or actresses who have played the character you choose. Free blog space is available at blogspot.com.

- Reza's stage directions call for the action of *The God of Carnage* to take place in "A living room. No realism. Nothing superfluous." Design a set for the play. You may sketch, draw, paint, build a three-dimensional model of, or create a collage of your ideal set. Along with your design, write a brief explanation of how you feel your set design is appropriate for the play and Reza's instructions.

Social Values

The meeting between the Vallons and Reilles takes place beneath the flag of upholding social values. Rather than squabble in court, the parents have decided that their reasonableness as adults will be enough to find a satisfying compromise. Determined to act civil, they make small talk over espresso and cake, congratulating themselves on their politesse. Véronique is especially firm in her belief that the values of Western society hinge on peacekeeping and personal growth. Michel demonstrates these values in action by pretending to care as much as his wife does about the meeting, avoiding conflict through playacting agreement. Annette, too, is willing to make a show of refined manners, but Alain breaks the rules immediately by taking calls on his cell phone. This rude behavior suggests that the meeting is not important to him, and he quickly admits that, in fact, it is not. He is the most honest about his disinterest because, as a rich, white male, he is allowed more leeway in society to break the rules.

His dismissal of the meeting's importance infuriates Véronique, who is a social crusader and enforcer of civility, but Véronique, too, steps over the line of polite society when she demands to know how Ferdinand will be punished, essentially telling the Reilles how to raise their child correctly. As the two dominant spouses, Alain and Véronique represent opposite philosophies of civilization. Véronique believes in fairness, equality, and compassion, while Alain believes in the god of carnage: the instincts to kill, steal, and exploit for personal gain. As pettiness and egotism gradually replace the couples' desire to uphold a façade of pleasantness, the god of carnage is set loose in the room. Each character spirals out of control, emerging from their disguises as good, reasonable, and respectful adults to reveal their grotesque true forms: childish, rampaging monsters with no concern for anyone but themselves.

Violence

Violence is the ultimate force in the play. The couples gather to settle the aftermath of violence between their sons only to be consumed by violence themselves. Véronique's insistence that people are good and that society brings individuals closer in a positive way is drowned out by the beating of war drums in her own living room. In fact, she is the most physically violent of the group, attacking her husband in a blind rage that makes Alain—high priest of carnage—laugh and declare after an hour of bitter argument that he likes her. Violence comes in all forms in the play: an attack with a stick, single combat, the presumed death of a hamster, the horrific reality of Darfur, shredded tulips, a destroyed phone, vomiting, verbal abuse, a scuffle over a bottle of rum, a purse hurled against the door, and the list goes on. Violence, not peace, is the characters' true nature, for when the trappings of polite society fall away, the violent tendencies of each character are unleashed full force. Véronique's goal of finding a compromise between families is revealed as a self-serving interest in stroking her own ego as a peacekeeper. Alain and Michel glory in the memory of their own schoolyard gangs, revealing their bias. Annette is too exhausted from the solitude of her child rearing, left alone while Alain ignores their family in favor of an affair with his telephone. She simply agrees to Véronique's requests, trying to speed the process up. The peace process is hopeless in such a gathering of greed, disillusionment, cowardice, and narcissism.

In Medias Res

To start a work of literature in medias res means to start in the middle of the situation rather than from the beginning. *The God of Carnage* begins in medias res as Véronique is reading a statement describing the attack aloud to the Reilles. Rather than begin the play with the attack itself (the true origin of the drama) or at the beginning of the meeting, the in medias res introduction has all four parents seated in the Vallons's living room discussing the incident. Reza uses this technique to obscure the details of the attack, so that aspects of the incident (for example, "armed" versus "furnished") are up for debate. Like the parents, the audience is not present for the attack, learning only by word of mouth what happened. Without any witnesses to the event present, either in the characters or the audience, the only descriptions given of the attack are subjective—told through the eyes of the parents who are searching for blame.

Monologue

A monologue is a speech given by a single character in a drama. For example, Annette gives a lengthy, uninterrupted monologue on the subject of masculinity after the men give up their effort to save Alain's phone. After announcing that everyone feels better now that the phone is dead, she tells an anecdote about seeing an attractive man carrying a shoulder bag and finding him instantly undesirable. She believes a man should have an air of solitude, not be attached to an accessory like a phone or shoulder bag. Another example of a monologue is Véronique's reassurance of her daughter at the end of the play. Her long list of what the hamster will eat in the wild strikes a positive, healing note after so much destruction, though she reveals after hanging up that she does not believe a word of what she has just said. Monologues highlight a character's state of mind, personality, and patterns of speech, as they become the temporary focal point of the audience and other characters.

Darfur Tragedy

Considered by the United Nations to be the world's worst humanitarian crisis, the situation in Darfur is the result of the combination of several factors. After Sudan gained independence from British and Anglo-Egyptian rule in 1956, political chaos and civil war ravaged the country. In addition to endemic political instability, a devastating drought in the 1980s caused desertification of previously farmable land and resulted in ongoing famine. In 2002, before the outbreak of war, the population of the Darfur region of Sudan was estimated at six million, the majority of whom were farmers organized into groups on tracts of land called Dar. Traditionally the farmers of a Dar share the land with one another as well as with nomads who travel seasonally with their livestock. However, following the drought, tensions between farmers and nomads rose, as competition for fertile land grew heated. This discontent, fostered by the neglect of the Darfur region by the Sudanese government and the exploitation of Darfur's resources and its people by neighboring Libya, began to fester. Darfurians felt the Sudanese government in Khartoum ignored their increasingly desperate situation. Rebel groups began to form.

In February of 2003, the escalating tensions

between the government and two rebel groups in particular—the Sudan Liberation Army (SLA) and the Justice and Equality Movement (JEM)—finally snapped as rebel forces attacked the al-Fashir airport. In response, the Sudanese government created the Janjawid, a militia recruited for the purpose of destroying the rebellion by any means necessary. The result has been the death of three hundred thousand Darfurians and the displacement of two million refugees. The international community was outraged by the atrocities committed by the Sudanese army and Janjawid, but Sudan has resisted much of the peacekeeping efforts. The United Nations International Criminal Court issued a warrant for Sudanese president Omer al-Bashir's arrest in March 2009, on charges of genocide and crimes against humanity.

The Bourgeoisie

In France, the middle class is also known as the bourgeoisie, making up more than half the population. First rising to prominence in the early to mid-1800s as the result of the advances of the Industrial Revolution, the bourgeoisie drive consumerist culture, seeking out material pleasures such as home furnishings, technology, and fashion. With a better education than the lower class, the bourgeoisie value participation in and knowledge of politics. Members of the bourgeoisie have time and energy to devote to changing the world around them for the better through activism, rather than spending their time in the act of daily survival, as is a necessity for those in the lower class, who cannot make ends meet. Concerning the early development of the strong social values of the bourgeoisie, Peter Stearns writes in "The Rise of the Middle Classes" in *European Society in Upheaval*: "They agreed that the family was the proper basis for society and the goal of economic effort. They agreed that sons should be give a good start in life, through … education and a solid inheritance." The bourgeoisie are culturally and politically engaged and often take an active part in shaping their society and upholding its values.

Critical Overview

The God Of Carnage debuted to positive reviews, winning the 2009 Tony Award for Best Play as well as the 2009 Laurence Olivier Award for Best Comedy. Susannah Clapp writes in "Are You Sitting Uncomfortably?" for the London *Guardian* in praise of Reza's "singular theatrical shocks, shrewd circumstantial detail and soliloquies that give [actors] a moment in the sun with a big central subject."

Many critics note that while the play's text may at times seem dark, the stage brings the eccentricities and inherent humor in the couples' irreconcilable differences to light. Elysa Gardner calls the play "scabrously funny," in her review for *USA Today*, going on to say: "It's just a matter of time before the meeting devolves into an orgy of verbal and physical brawling—and a showcase for first-rate ensemble acting." As a critique of middle-class values, the critics agree unanimously that *The God of Carnage* delivers a gut punch. In her review of the play for the London *Independent*, Alice Jones writes: "Reza has proved that she can skewer the middle classes like no other, revelling in the grotesque prejudices not only of her characters but also of the audience."

The combination of dark humor and subject matter that touches on the common fears of its audience results in new heights of hilarity as social nightmares (vomiting, crying, name calling, and tantrums) come to life. Terry Teachout writes in "Beating Up the Bourgeoisie" for the *Wall Street Journal*: "Reza is back on Broadway with another of her slightly pretentious, consummately effective comedies of middle-class manners.... By the play's end ... the audience has laughed itself well past silly." As the couples' attempts at civility are shredded like Véronique's tulips, the audience sees what lies beneath the characters's adult identities: children just as brutal and unapologetic as their sons. Lucy Komisar writes in her review for the *Komisar Scoop*: "Reza's *God of Carnage* smartly shows the disintegration of the thin veneer of civilization that keeps people civil." *The God of Carnage* delights in the slow descent of the Reilles and Vallons from respectable, worldly citizens to violent beasts. Ben Brantley writes in "Rumble in the Living Room" for the *New York Times*: "A study in the tension between civilized surface and savage instinct, this play ... is itself a satisfyingly primitive entertainment with an intellectual veneer."

What Do I Read Next?

- In Elizabeth Ross's young-adult novel *Belle Epoque* (2013), a desperate runaway in Paris answers an ad to serve as a plain friend to make the daughter of a countess seem more beautiful by comparison. Yet as Maude learns the secrets of Parisian society and the family she serves, keeping her secret becomes an impossible challenge.

- In Reza's first play, *Conversations after a Burial* (2000), six mourners gather after the burial of a man to discuss his life and death. Each has a unique perspective on Simon Weinberg's life, whether siblings, spouses, friends, or lovers, and each is allowed in their grief to recall the

Simon they knew and loved best.

- A dinner party between two couples turns disastrous in Ayad Akhtar's Pulitzer Prize–winning play *Disgraced* (2012). The four successful friends—Amir, an ex-Muslim lawyer battling with internalized Islamophobia following the September 11 terrorist attacks; his wife, Emily; his colleague Jory; and Jory's husband, Isaac—quickly become embattled across lines of race, class, religion, and politics, as opinions are taken personally and lead to devastating revelations of betrayal.

- Timothy Murray's *Mimesis, Masochism, and Mime: The Politics of Theatricality in Contemporary French Thought* (1997) collects essays by leading voices in literature and philosophy of the effects of theater on French culture.

- In *Who's Afraid of Virginia Woolf?*, by Edward Albee (1962), George and Martha invite a young couple into their home for a night of mind games and cruel manipulations that blur the line between fantasy and reality.

- *Lord of the Flies*, by William Golding (1954), portrays the collapse of the values of Western society through the adventures of a small band of boys who are stranded on a remote island following a plane crash. The spirit of cooperation and optimism soon gives way to fear and violence as the boys turn to increasingly brutal means of survival.

- Two men wait by a tree in *Waiting for Godot*, by Samuel Beckett (1953). Bored, they speak in circles, carrying on surreal conversations that seem at once senseless and somehow profound. Those who pass by say that Godot is coming, and the characters believe that Godot will make things better, but Godot never comes. This masterpiece of the Theater of the Absurd showcases the genre's emphasis on minimalism and the gaps in communication—what is lost, misunderstood, and altered when two people attempt to connect through language.

- In *Topdog/Underdog*, by Suzan-Lori Parks (2001), two brothers, ironically named Lincoln and Booth, are pitted against each other in a decades-long sibling rivalry felt all the more acutely in the fact that they are each other's only family. After their parents abandoned them as children, they grew up reliant on each other. As adults, they must navigate the influence of outside forces alongside their own expectations of how they should carry themselves in the world.

- *No Exit*, by Jean-Paul Sartre (1944), features three characters trapped together in a room in Hell as punishment following their deaths. Expecting to be tortured by demons for their sins, the characters soon realize that they will be each other's torturers, their opinions and desires forever at odds in a room without escape.

Sources

Brantley, Ben, "Rumble In The Living Room," In *New York Times*, June 6, 2010, http://www.nytimes.com/2009/03/23/theater/reviews_r=0 (accessed June 15, 2016).

"Carnage (2011)," imbd.com, http://www.imdb.com/title/tt1692486/ (accessed June 15, 2016).

Clapp, Susannah, "Are You Sitting Uncomfortably?," in *Guardian* (London, England), March 30, 2008, https://www.theguardian.com/stage/2008/mar/30/the (accessed June 15, 2016).

Corder, Mike, "Omar al-Bashir Charged by Hague for Orchestrating Darfur Genocide," in *Christian Science Monitor*, July 12, 2010, http://www.csmonitor.com/From-thenews-wires/2010/0712/Omar-al-Bashir-charged-by-Haguefor-orchestrating-Darfur-genocide (accessed June 20, 2016).

Fukuyama, Francis, "The Middle-Class Revolution," in *Wall Street Journal*, June 28, 2013, http://www.wsj.com/articles/SB1000142412788732: (accessed June 20, 2016).

Gardner, Elysa, "God of Carnage, Blithe Spirit Lifting Spirits on Broadway," in *USA Today*, March 23, 2016, http://usatoday30.usatoday.com/life/theater/reviews/

22-carnage-blithe_N.htm (accessed June 15, 2016).

Giguere, Amanda, *The Plays of Yasmina Reza on the English and American Stage*, MacFarland, 2010, pp. 5–11, 116–49.

Jones, Alice, "God of Carnage, Gielgud Theatre, London," in *Independent* (London, England), March 26, 2008, http://www.independent.co.uk/arts-entertainment/theatre-dance/reviews/god-of-carnage-gielgud-theatrelondon-801139.html (accessed June 15, 2016).

Komisar, Lucy, "The God of Carnage Watches Polite Society Disintegrate," in *The Komisar Scoop*, October 2009, http://www.thekomisarscoop.com/2009/10/the-godof-carnage-watches-polite-society-disintegrate/ (accessed June 15, 2016).

Reza, Yasmina, *God of Carnage*, translated by Christopher Hampton, Faber and Faber, 2008.

Sikainga, Ahmad, "'The World's Worst Humanitarian Crisis': Understanding the Darfur Conflict," in *Origins*, Vol. 2, No. 5, February 2009, http://origins.osu.edu/article/worlds-worst-humanitarian-crisis-understandingdarfur-conflict (accessed June 20, 2016).

Spencer, Charles, "God of Carnage: Electrifying, Despite Lights Failing," in *Telegraph* (London, England), March 26, 2008, http://www.telegraph.co.uk/culture/theatre/drama/36 of-Carnage-Electrifying-despitelights-failing.html (accessed June 15, 2016).

Stearns, Peter, "The Rise of the Middle Classes," in *Euro-pean Society in Upheaval*, 1967, pp. 117–133, http://history.tamu.edu/faculty/resch/Stearns,%20Eai (accessed June 20, 2016).

Teachout, Terry, "Beating Up the Bourgeoisie," in *Wall Street Journal*, March 27, 2009, http://www.wsj.com/articles/SB1238102502143516: (accessed June 15, 2016).

Venturi, Richard, "Up against the Wall: The French and American Middle Classes," in *France Stratégie*, February 2016, http://www.strategie.gouv.fr/sites/strategie.gouv.fr/fi (accessed June 20, 2016).

Waal, Alex de, "Tragedy in Darfur," in *Boston Review*, October 5, 2004, http://www.bostonreview.net/de-waaltragedy-in-darfur (accessed June 20, 2016).

Further Reading

Bradby, David, *Modern French Drama: 1940–1990*, Cambridge University Press, 1991.

> This volume traces the history of the theater from World War II to 1990, touching not only on influential literary superstars of the time, such as Samuel Beckett and Arthur Adamov, but also on the work of talented but lesser-known playwrights. A bibliography and blackand-white photos are included.

Finburgh, C., and C. Lavery, *Contemporary French Theatre and Performance*, Palgrave Macmillan, 2011.

> This collection of essays explores the relationship of French theater to the nation's culture and history, covering both traditional and experimental performances as well as the specific influence of individual playwrights. Topics include the translation of text to stage, the effect of economy and politics on the theater, feminism, the role of dance and poetry, and amateur and street performances.

Reza, Yasmina, *'Art,'* Farrar, Straus, and Giroux, 1997.

In Reza's Tony Award–winning play, a man buys a pure white painting for a ludicrous sum of money, to the utter disbelief of his closest friends. A dark comedy that skewers modern conceptions of art and its value, the play also exposes the fault lines often present but overlooked within friendships, to disastrous, hilarious results.

Turk, Edward Baron, *French Theatre Today: The View from New York, Paris, and Avignon*, University of Iowa Press, 2011.

This study of French theater uses the author's attendance of over 150 performances over the course of a single year to draw conclusions about the state of twenty-first-century French theater: its relationship to the audience, its innovations and traditions, as well as the ways in which it reflects and distorts the society that surrounds it.

Suggested Search Terms

Yasmina Reza

The God of Carnage

Yasmina Reza AND The God of Carnage

The God of Carnage AND drama

Yasmina Reza AND Tony Award

Yamina Reza AND Christopher Hampton

The God of Carnage AND violence

middle-class manners AND plays

Darfur, Sudan

Milton Keynes UK
Ingram Content Group UK Ltd.
UKHW020630130923
428592UK00014B/452

9 780270 528466